Inspiring
Women
Every Day

G000025362

September

FRIENDS

....

RACHEL HALL-SMITH

October

A RESILIENT LIFE

....

DIANE REGAN

Plus... 'Be Inspired' article, CWR Today
pages and CWR Ministry Events

Rachel Hall-Smith

Rachel began writing for Inspiring Women in 2013, and was delighted to make her first visit to Waverley Abbey House last year. She chooses to spend her free time singing in a choir, leading worship, preaching, writing, visiting the theatre and walking – all of which are greatly enhanced when enjoyed with family and dear friends.

Diane Regan

Diane and her husband Patrick are the founders of Kintsugi Hope, a charity that seeks to promote the understanding and acceptance of emotional and mental health. As part of their work in equipping churches to support their communities, they host conferences across the UK on all aspects of our wellbeing. Diane and Patrick live in Essex with their four children, two dogs and a very tolerant cat.

Copyright © CWR 2020. Published by CWR, Waverley Abbey House, Waverley Lane, Farnham, Surrey GU9 8EP, UK. Tel: 01252 784700 Email: mail@cwr.org.uk Registered Charity No. 294387. Registered Limited Company No. 1990308. Front cover image: Stocksy/Ania Boniecka
Concept development, editing, design and production by CWR. Printed in England by Linney. All rights reserved. No part of this publication may be reproduced, stored in a retrieval system, or transmitted, in any form or by any means, electronic, mechanical, photocopying, recording or otherwise, without the prior permission in writing of CWR.
Unless otherwise indicated, all Scripture references are from the Holy Bible, New International Version® Anglicised, NIV® Copyright © 1979, 1984, 2011 by Biblica, Inc.® Used by permission. All rights reserved worldwide.

Friends

RACHEL HALL-SMITH

T his September in the UK, thousands of children will be preparing to return to school for a brand-new academic year. Having adapted to home-schooling earlier in the year in response to the Covid-19 pandemic, most will no doubt be looking forward to catching up with old friends and meeting the new kids joining their class. Whatever our own situation in life (single, married, divorced or widowed), we've each experienced friendships. These may have been fleeting or enduring; happy or sad experiences – most likely a combination. At their best, friendships are enjoyable and enriching, becoming a significant part of our lives.

Although the biblical accounts of human friendships often lack detail, we can learn much from the overriding principles within Scripture. We begin with our reading from Matthew today, so that we can start from the premise that if we love God first and then others as much as ourselves, we'll be better friends and have healthier friendships.

From the Genesis account of creation, we see that God didn't intend for us to be alone. Charles Kingsley (1819–1875), the priest and novelist, said, 'A blessed thing it is for any man or woman to have a friend; one human soul whom we can trust utterly; who knows the best and worst of us, and who loves us in spite of all our faults'. Leisure activities are usually more fun when the pleasure is shared with others and it's great to unwind together, chat and chill over a coffee or meal. There's camaraderie in working or ministering together too. But what's even more amazing is that our creator God has actually chosen you and me to be *His* friends.

Matthew 22:34–40

'Teacher, which is the greatest commandment in the Law?' (v36)

For prayer and reflection

Father, guide my thoughts as I consider the friendships I value and the kind of friend that I am. Teach me how to enhance my relationships. Amen.

God's friend

'The LORD would speak to Moses face to face, as one speaks to a friend.' (v11)

When we're in the garden, country or at the seaside, we can marvel at the beauty of a creator God. And, as we pray the Lord's Prayer, we acknowledge He's our Father and that we're His adopted children. But today we're focusing on the amazing fact that He also calls us His friends!

In the Old Testament, God refers to both Moses and Abraham in this way (Isa. 41:8). In the New Testament, it is Jesus who expresses how our Father sees us: 'When Jesus saw their faith, he said, "Friend, your sins are forgiven"' (Luke 5:20). He is our Saviour and we're saved by grace through faith. And, although we can't see Him physically, we live in His presence. Ephesians 2:6 teaches that 'God raised us up with Christ and seated us with him in the heavenly realms in Christ Jesus'.

As a friend of God, I primarily liken my closeness with Him to that between a father and child, but the level of intimacy can be deeper than that experienced in any human friendship. We're unable to wear a mask to hide our imperfections from Him and there's no need. While we speak to the Lord, as the Lord spoke with Moses, we are clothed in His righteousness. We can have great friendships with each other, but none can bring a satisfaction and completeness like a relationship with God. God can never fail us.

The book of Revelation reveals the outcome of God's friendship. 'Look! God's dwelling-place is now among the people, and he will dwell with them. They will be his people, and *God himself will be with them* and be their God' (Rev. 21:3, my emphasis). What an amazing hope we have.

Does your soul genuinely thirst for His friendship?

For prayer and reflection

My Father and friend, thank You for Your awesome love. Draw me deeper into Your heart. In the name of Jesus, I pray. Amen.

Friends **of Jesus**

John 15:9–17

'I no longer call you servants… I have called you friends' (v15)

I n the dining room of some holiday accommodation I once stayed in, there was a picture of the owner's son casually standing with the Duke and Duchess of Cambridge. At first, it's easy to think that I don't have such illustrious friends. Except I do! Jesus came to offer me the privileged relationship of 'friend'. By rights, 'servanthood' is all I could have expected. Jesus was perfect and He chose to surrender His own life for future friendship with imperfect human beings.

What an immense debt we owe Him for His sacrificial love. When He commands us to love each other, as He does on multiple occasions in this passage, our response should be out of pure gratitude. If Jesus is our friend, then we should want to be more like Him. And Jesus *loves*.

You're probably familiar with the hymn *What a Friend We Have in Jesus*, written by Joseph M. Scriven (1819–1886). It started life as a poem written to comfort his mum (who was living in Ireland while he was in Canada). In verse two we find these words: 'Can we find a friend so faithful, who will all our sorrows share?' The answer to this rhetorical question is certainly 'No!' As we take all our worries and discouragement to Jesus in prayer we find a refuge of peace.

We *can* feel secure, valued and happy in human friendship (and in a romantic relationship or Christian community), but this is no substitute for spending time in God's presence. And, as we do that, we can pray for His blessing on our friends. If a companion is yet to come to faith in Jesus, let's ask Him to enable us to share our faith in a sensitive way, at an appropriate time.

For prayer and reflection

Thank You, Jesus, that You are my ultimate friend. I'm so grateful for Your sacrificial love which cost You so much. Help me to share our friendship with others. Amen.

Choosing friends

2 Corinthians
6:14–18

'what does a believer have in common with an unbeliever?' (v15)

This passage contains crucial advice for a woman choosing a husband. But it's also helpful when considering how to select our best mates. Think about the last time you fostered a new friendship. Often we start interacting with someone new as we share activities (hobbies, church, socialising), then chats, moans and laughter flow into sharing thoughts and feelings. Consider what kind of influence that friendship has since had on your life. Now reflect on it from a different angle... Why do you think your friend chose you?

Today's passage contains five similarly challenging questions, with the aim of warning us to be on our guard. Two Old Testament Proverbs are worth recalling here: 'Many curry favour with a ruler, and everyone is the friend of one who gives gifts' (19:6); and, 'One who has unreliable friends soon comes to ruin, but there is a friend who sticks closer than a brother' (18:24).

In John Bunyan's allegory *The Pilgrim's Progress*, the protagonist, Christian, experienced a wide variety of 'friends' during his journey of faith. Some seemed negative and insincere but his closest companions – Faithful and Hopeful – were dependable, honest, loyal and encouraging. (You could check out their visit to Doubting Castle.)

Like Christian, I've chosen to live for Jesus, so my closest friends have the same goal – which is to become more Christlike and to share His kingdom. That doesn't mean to say that I have no non-Christian friends, as I enjoy companionship with those of other faiths or none. But it's good to pray when establishing and developing their friendship.

For prayer and reflection

Reflect on 1 Samuel 16:7: 'The Lord does not look at the things people look at. People look at the outward appearance, but the Lord looks at the heart.'

CWR Ministry Events

Please pray for the team

DATE	EVENT	PLACE	PRESENTER(S)
4–6 Sep	Inspiring Women Autumn Weekend: Journeying with God through Transitional Times	Waverley Abbey House	Beverley Shepherd and : the Inspiring Women team
29 Sep	Great Chapters of the Bible: The Counter Cultural Wisdom of God that Changes the World	WAH	Philip Greenslade
21 Oct	Inspiring Women Autumn Day: What the Bible Says About Women	WAH	Elizabeth Hodkinson
20–22 Oct	Bible Discovery: With Jesus in the Upper Room – Reflections on John 13–17	WAH	Philip Greenslade

We hope to be 'post-lockdown', running courses and welcoming back our new and returning students to Waverley Abbey College after the summer break, following significant adaptions to remote studying earlier in the year. Please pray for 'business as usual', and for staff and students to be blessed as they begin or resume their studies.

We would also appreciate prayer for our ongoing ministry in Singapore and Cambodia, as well as the many regional events that we hope will be back up and running around the UK this year.

For further information and a full list of CWR's courses, seminars and events, call **(+44) 01252 784719** or visit **cwr.org.uk/courses**

You can also download our free Prayer Track, which includes daily prayers, from **cwr.org.uk/prayertrack**

Weekend

Be proactive

....

Romans 12:9–21

'Honour one another above yourselves.' (v10)

E ach weekend throughout this month, we'll focus on the 'one another' verses that equipped the Early Church community. These offer constructive advice for relationship building, which enabled them (and will help us) to develop sound friendships.

I did a search of the New Testament to discover that there are 59 'one another' quotes. It was an interesting exercise to analyse and evaluate them. I discovered that they largely fall into four main categories – love, humility, unity and edifying verses – and that the 'Love one another' verses were in the majority by far. (We'll discuss some of these next weekend.)

'Honour one another' is at the hub of each of these categories. So, how do we honour someone? It's to *esteem* them; show them *respect*; make them feel *valued*. It's to endow them with *dignity*.

But how do we honour someone practically? Loyalty and confidentiality are two ways, but each of our friends is unique. Let's spend time this weekend thinking and praying about how we can pay tribute to them, individually.

....

Optional further reading

1 Thessalonians 3:11–13; 1 Peter 3:8–12

His **inner** circle

Matthew 4:18–22

"'Come, follow me,' Jesus said' (v19)

Jesus was a friend of sinners, but He also had an inner circle. At the beginning of His public ministry, we see Him drawing a team of 12 together to be His disciples and for companionship and support. Three of the four men He recruited – Peter, James and John – were to become particularly close friends of His. They accompanied Jesus as He was 'transfigured' – shining like the sun as He talked to Moses and Elijah (Matt. 17). That must have been a mind-blowing shared experience! But they were also by His side at His lowest point (in Gethsemane).They were to journey with their friend through His capture and crucifixion.

Jesus' best friend was John (13:23) and it's the Gospel of John we'll turn to see how Jesus demonstrated His love to His friends – by doing the job of a servant (John 13:1–13). Jesus' seemingly menial action of washing His friends' feet stunned Peter and it provides us with a stark contrast to some of the worldly friendships we observe today. Sadly, these can be about 'pleasing ourselves' and a 'me, me, me' mentality. Paul gives us this advice: 'You... were called to be free. But do not use your freedom to indulge the flesh; rather, serve one another humbly in love' (Gal. 5:13). Jesus' friends failed Him in Gethsemane, falling asleep when He needed them to watch and pray. It is better if we choose to display the commitment of Jesus in our friendships.

Jeff Lucas, in a past issue of his Bible reading notes *Life Every Day*, once commented: 'The mighty Son of God needed His friends. And so do we. Let's make sure that we invest in friendships that will stand the test of time.' Amen.

For prayer and reflection

Lord, make me willing and able to demonstrate my love and Your love to my friends. Amen.

A friendship **motto**

Matthew 7:9–12

'do to others what you would have them do to you' (v12)

ave you seen the 1992 Disney film *Aladdin*? Genie sings a song called *Friend Like Me*, where he promises to give Aladdin anything he wants. Jesus, in today's Bible reading, is not advising us to be like Genie, but to consider the needs of our friends above our own. He's advocating a two-way relationship where both parties act selflessly. This is the opposite of being needy and dependent – which is what Genie is inferring Aladdin should be!

Let's consider the characteristics of a 'selfless' friend. A deep friendship cannot be built in the ten minutes' coffee time after church, so I'd suggest that giving of our *time* is key. It's easy to pack our schedules with commitments, so we may need to deliberately make it a priority. Are we willing to clear our diary at short notice for a friend in need? Be ready to offer a listening ear (Prov. 18:13), remembering that a sensitive silence can be more appropriate than a light-hearted comment.

However, a good friend is also prepared to speak the truth, even if it's hard to do so. Sharing and understanding another's struggles and doubts, without judgment and in confidence, is an expression of genuine empathy. And a selfless friend takes the opportunity to encourage and affirm, both in the good times and the bad.

Sometimes it can take an act of our will to set aside our own troubles and 'be there' for our friends. (After all, I've had a rough day and it's just downright unfair.) But, as we encourage them, faith and hope will also rise in our own hearts to address our own situations. And, if we act in this way, our friends will be a lot better from having us by their side!

For prayer and reflection

Reflect on Hebrews 3:13: 'But encourage one another daily, as long as it is called "Today".'

Chatting amongst friends

James 3:7–18

'no human being
can tame the
tongue.' (v8)

t's possible to ruin even a close friendship by chatting unwisely to others (Prov. 17:9). Has this ever happened to you? How would you do things differently if you could rewind the situation? And have you ever discovered that sending negative or unwise texts or emails on impulse can have a similar outcome? The wisdom conveyed in our reading from James today, if put into practice, could help protect our precious friendships.

Note the strong words used in verse eight to describe the destructive power of the tongue. Then spot where cursing, boasting and lying are listed. Elsewhere in Scripture, we find that slandering (James 4:11), grumbling (James 5:9), gossiping (Prov. 16:28) and judging others (Rom. 14:13) are soundly condemned too. But let's reread verses 17–18 and make a list of the characteristics of *wise* conversation.

Now think of the topics and tone of your verbal exchanges with friends. Do they match up to your list? Whether we're discussing the plotline of a television drama or the Sunday morning teaching; whether we're being frivolous or serious, our words shouldn't be careless or detrimental to others. When we're expressing our opinions or feelings, let's consider the impact they might have before we air them.

When we view Jesus together with His friends in the Gospels, we see Him imparting divine insight, encouragement and correction, all in a spirit of love. So, 'let us consider how we may spur one another on towards love and good deeds' (Heb. 10:24). And let's also not hesitate to say 'sorry' when we need to!

For prayer and reflection

Lord, forgive me for the times when reckless words have not been in my friends' best interests. Help me to speak with less haste and greater consideration in the future. Amen.

Loneliness

Luke 15:11–16

'He longed to fill his stomach with the pods… the pigs were eating, but no one gave him anything.' (v16)

We all experience loneliness at some stage in our lives – perhaps more so this year than ever before! Like the son in this story, I left my family (in 1985). But, unlike him, it was to train for a career rather than live indulgently! I found myself in a highly populated but anonymous city. The son probably had 'fair weather' friends when he squandered his wealth, as fake friends will often have their own agenda. I had no friends, but that, I suppose, was better than having bad ones – as Proverbs 13:20 says 'for a companion of fools suffers harm'. But it sure didn't feel like it!

In 2020, technology can easily become a substitute for personal contact. Organisations use pre-recorded telephone messages to suggest going 'online' when what we really want is to is talk to somebody. Often, we define a 'friend' as a contact on a social networking website. When you feel isolated, take encouragement from the many stories of how in His time on earth, Jesus offered friendship to those whom no one else did. Be the one to make contact first! And remember – social media can be incredibly effective for reaching out to people who are also isolated. The recent Covid-19 outbreak will no doubt have produced countless stories of this. And it's great for maintaining established contacts, too!

Large congregations can sometimes be impersonal, so if this is your experience at church, consider joining a small group (home group, ministry team etc). You could also seek friendships with those on the margins of your church. They may welcome company as much as you.

If you're praying for new friendships, talk to God and believe that He will guide you. When I did this in 1985, someone I knew moved into the area, and I had a friend.

For prayer and reflection

Thank You, God, that You are ever by my side. May I be sensitive to someone's loneliness and quick to befriend. Amen.

Devotion

Ruth 1:6–22

'Where you go I will go, and where you stay I will stay.' (v16)

I f you asked me: which Bible character I'd like to have as a friend, I'd definitely request Ruth! Her name means 'loyal friend' and I can tell from her story that she'd be there for me whatever may happen and at any time of day or night.

United in grief by the death of their husbands, Ruth adopted her mother-in-law Naomi's faith and community (v16) and this was central to their friendship. They'd shared love and motivation.

In Bethlehem, Ruth, as the fitter, younger person, provided for Naomi's physical needs. She didn't slack. She followed Naomi's advice, acknowledging the wisdom she'd gained though age and experience. And God saw Ruth's loyalty and honoured her every step of the way. I feel her life is a beautiful demonstration of the characteristics we should hope to be producing: 'the fruit of the Spirit is love... forbearance, kindness, goodness, faithfulness, gentleness and self-control' (Gal. 5:22–23). Our friendships will be healthier if we follow Ruth's example of loyalty, too.

Paul advocates that we 'Rejoice with those who rejoice' and 'mourn with those who mourn' (Rom. 12:15). This empathy adds to the joy and comfort of our companions. Standing shoulder to shoulder in both the great times and the bad (evidenced in today's reading) is our calling. It was Jesus Himself who outlined the second 'Great Commandment' (Matt. 22:39) – to love our neighbour as ourselves. So it's even more true of our *friends*.

And it's worth remembering that if we, like Ruth, experience difficulties, then we're more able to help friends in a similar situation. It gives us credibility.

For prayer and reflection

When friends celebrate, may I show joy not jealousy. When they face loss, may they be strengthened as I stand by their side. Amen.

Weekend

Love one another

....

John 13:33–38

'By this everyone will know that you are my disciples' (v35).

God is love – it's His very essence (1 John 4:8). And to be loved is an essential human need. So, unsurprisingly, a key theme in Scripture is the call to love. It's clear from this weekend's Bible verses that God *initiates* love; that we need to *respond* to it and that we're called to *share* it.

The Greek language (in which the New Testament was first written) has several different words for 'love'. *Agape* is the word used in John 13. It describes 'divine love', which is unconditional, sacrificial, pure and giving. Another Greek word for 'love' is *philia*, which describes the warmth and affection between friends. Our openness and even shared laughter can transform people's lives and radiate God's love. It can influence future friends too!

We all know that loving others can be difficult at times. Even longstanding friends can disappoint. But His love can motivate and enable. So if you're feeling a bit 'let down' at present, let's choose to honour the name of our Father by opting for the path of love rather than the path of resentment.

....

Optional further reading

1 Corinthians 13; 1 John 4:7–21

Boundaries and barriers

T oday we consider some of the issues which prevent or hinder friendships from forming or developing. Whilst it's vital a marriage remains exclusive – please reread verse four – it needn't be threatened by a strong friendship outside the family unit. Indeed, it can be strengthened, as it's rare for one person to be able to meet all the human needs of another. As a wife myself, my female friends add a vital and enriching dimension to my life and my male friends are also friends of my husband.

Whilst marriage is exclusive, friendship is not (v2). Beware of church 'cliques' forming, perhaps unwittingly. One theme of our reading today is to *be welcoming*. If we feel usurped when a friend befriends another, we need to address our own feelings! And friendships are ever-changing. Friends move away (social media is useful here for staying in contact) and distance can be felt when our friends' experiences and priorities change, perhaps through marriage or starting a family, or a demanding new job.

Verse three of today's reading speaks of ministering to people in need. I've observed that it's possible to offer support to others but remain too private to develop friendships. If this challenges you, set out to enter your next social situation 'full on'! Prepare some 'starter questions': 'What have you been up to this week?' or 'Do you have any plans for...?' Then listen, be prepared to share and establish common ground. It's not about being nosy, but showing a genuine interest. By focusing on their (and your) 'doing', discussion on 'feeling' can follow.

Hebrews 13:1–4

'Keep on loving one another as... sisters.' (v1)

For prayer and reflection

Reflect on the words of the well-known hymn: 'Jesus knows our every weakness; take it to the Lord in prayer.'

Best friends

**1 Samuel
18:1–16**

'Jonathan became
one in spirit with
David, and he
loved him as
himself.' (v1)

I n children's fiction, Pooh has Piglet and Mowgli has Baloo. But when I consider 'best friends' in the Bible, it's Jonathan and David who immediately come to mind. Jonathan's father, Saul, was king – but God rejected him due to his rebellion (1 Sam. 15:23). However, it is not Jonathan who is his successor, but David, who is chosen by God and anointed (16:13). He operates in God's strength and blessing, and makes a covenant with Jonathan (makes a relationship of commitment before God). But difficult times are ahead, evidenced by Saul's jealousy, violence and scheming (18:21). Jonathan will have split loyalties – will he side with his father or his friend?

Check out verse 2 of chapter 19 to see the decision Jonathan makes. And his devotion goes further: 'Jonathan said to David, "Whatever you want me to do, I'll do for you"' (20:4).

Let's ask ourselves some questions: Are we keen to ensure the wellbeing of our friends? Would we act as their advocate if necessary? Can we be relied upon – fully? And, who could *we* call in an emergency?

Sadly, these two friends were forced apart. Twice David spared Saul's life (chapters 24 and 26), but was unable to prevent his and Jonathan's death when they fled from battle (31:2–4). If we read David's grief in 2 Samuel 1:26 it will prompt us not to take our friends for granted!

We see David's faithfulness continue – 'Is there anyone still left in the house of Saul to whom I can show kindness for Jonathan's sake' (2 Sam. 9:1) – as he welcomes Mephibosheth, Jonathan's son, into his household (a response to the covenant recorded in 1 Samuel 20:14–17).

Loyalty in friendship. What a precious gift!

For prayer
and reflection

**For meditation:
'A friend loves at
all times, and a
brother is born for
a time of adversity'
(Prov. 17:17).**

Vulnerability

Psalm 41:1–9

W hy is it that we put up barriers between ourselves and others? Are we ashamed to let down our guard, fearing that we may be judged? Have we experienced betrayal in the past and wish to shield ourselves? This psalm of David reflects the pain and loss which can be felt when a friendship goes sour. Verses 1–3 suggest to me that he may have been stabbed in the back (metaphorically speaking). Perhaps he would be justified in withdrawing and remaining wary of others?

'Even my close friend, someone I trusted, one who shared my bread, has turned against me.' (v9)

I've done little formal church pastoring, but one visit was particularly memorable. The lady felt she could only open her heart to one person – someone overseas whom she 'knew' solely via email. The anonymity of the situation helped her and, fortunately (on this occasion), her cyber-friend was genuine. But I found it sad.

If we can't foster personal relationships, then we sacrifice enjoying each other's company as well as the prospect of true friendship. Let's be honest: people are imperfect, so they'll disappoint us from time to time. We cannot prevent this from happening and it's hard to control our initial reaction, but we *can* decide how to respond. And with God's help a wise response can defuse the situation. Resentment and revenge are unhealthy. Romans 12:17–21 offers some pertinent advice, concluding: 'Do not be overcome by evil, but overcome evil with good'. And forgiveness is the epitome of good. (We'll be returning to this topic next week.)

If David had avoided intimate friendship as a consequence of this experience, he would have lost out big time.

For prayer and reflection

Father, help me not to retreat from people who disappoint or hurt me. May I learn to see them through Your eyes. Amen.

God's Plan for Your Wellbeing

Brand-new church resource from Dave Smith

The Oxford English Dictionary defines wellbeing as 'the state of being comfortable, healthy and happy'. Others talk of a sense of meaning, purpose, good mental health, satisfaction, or simply feeling well. However, statistics would imply – especially given recent world events – that many people do not 'feel well', reporting stress, being under immense pressure, and feeling overwhelmed. Key ways to improving our wellbeing require us to be aware of how we are doing in various areas of our lives, and seeing how we might take positive steps forward.

The Hebrew word *shalom* perfectly expresses God's passion and plan for our wellbeing. Wellbeing was God's idea and He has the best plan for us. In his brand-new resource for churches and individuals, church leader Dave Smith encourages us to think of our lives as having six different but interrelated 'tanks', almost as if we have dials on our life dashboards. He identifies these as Physical, Emotional, Spiritual, Relational, Vocational and Financial. Each are vital and all are connected; and as such, an increase or decrease in any one of these areas can impact one or all of the others. To help illustrate all of these aspects of our wellbeing, Dave touches on the story of Elijah.

So wherever you may feel you are at – whether stressed,

overwhelmed, or simply seeking greater wellbeing in any area of your life – the Bible provides a wealth of insight on wellbeing, and how we can find health, wholeness and harmony with God, ourselves and others.

God's Plan for Your Wellbeing brilliantly highlights the overview of the Bible when it comes to wellbeing, looking at:

- Perfect Wellbeing (the first human beings made in the image of God);
- Lost Wellbeing (humanity turning their backs on God);
- Promised Wellbeing (new covenants between God and His people);
- Restored Wellbeing (Jesus' birth, death and resurrection);
- Increasing Wellbeing (the Holy Spirit's invitation);
- Complete Wellbeing (on Jesus' return).

This resource includes a book offering 50 daily readings with opportunities to reflect and respond, along with free online resources that provide group videos, discussions and sermon outlines, making it ideal for you, your small group or your whole church. All available from October.

Provisional cover

To register, buy the book or find out more, visit cwr.org.uk/wellbeing or use the order form at the back of these notes.

A problem **shared**

Luke 1:39–56

'Mary stayed with Elizabeth for about three months and then returned home.' (v56)

The song *With a little help from my friends* was written by Paul McCartney and John Lennon for their fellow Beatles bandmate Ringo Starr. Along life's journey, we will all find ourselves in need of support from time to time, but do we have friends we can trust with confidential information?

In today's reading, Mary turns to Elizabeth for support. Both women were unexpectedly expecting! Elizabeth's predicament was that she was elderly and her husband had strangely lost his voice, whilst Mary was to be an unmarried mum – and the mother of the long-awaited Messiah at that! But God gave them each other, and sharing a common predicament can forge a special friendship.

From the time that Elizabeth's baby leapt in her womb at Mary's arrival, I believe that Elizabeth was equipped by the Holy Spirit to encourage and prepare her for the uncertain times ahead. Proverbs 27:9 states 'the pleasantness of a friend springs from their heartfelt advice'. We trust in God but a little human wisdom and reassurance can go a long way.

Many of us will be familiar with the saying: 'A problem shared is a problem halved'. In Acts 24, we see that even the great St Paul was blessed by friends to take care of his needs (v23). Who is the Lord prompting *us* to support... and how?

A lovely postscript to this story is that Elizabeth's son John later described Mary's son, Jesus, as his friend: 'The friend who attends the bridegroom waits and listens for him, and is full of joy when he hears the bridegroom's voice. That joy is mine...' (John 3:29).

For prayer and reflection

Father, please help me to be sensitive to the needs of my friends. Show me what would be most helpful and supportive when the need arises. Amen.

Friends within the **family**

Friends are largely chosen but can be found in our family too. I don't have a sister but regard my daughter, who now has three children of her own, as a best friend.

In today's reading, I notice the strong bond between these sisters. Preachers usually highlight their differences (Luke 10:38–42), but their relationship was nothing like that of Leah and Rachel who had too much in common to be friends – they shared a husband! By contrast, let's recognise Martha and Mary's oneness of heart. Martha had opened their home to Jesus and His friendship was central to their own (John 11:5). Although responding differently – Martha going out to meet Jesus and Mary grieving privately (resentfully?) at home – they were united in pleading with their friend.

Subsequently, as Jesus brought Lazarus back to life, I wonder whether their initial responses were again different. Jesus reached beyond merely comforting them to bestowing restoration and unbelievable joy. Although this was a miraculous occurrence, we can view it as a personal challenge to bring God's blessings into the lives of others. In the midst of life's routine, how might we be creative in finding ways to do that?

From Martha and Mary's story, we see that friends can be different but unified. Their mutual relationship with Jesus gave them a togetherness which Leah and Rachel did not have. Let these accounts spur us on to value the friendships within our families and to guard against anything which could damage or destroy that affection. And for those of us without strong family ties, let's adopt a friend from our spiritual family.

John 11:1–3, 17–35

'So the sisters sent word to Jesus, "Lord, the one you love is ill."' (v3)

For prayer and reflection

Father, as I sit at Your feet, I pray that You will bless my family friends and protect the closeness we share. Amen.

Be tolerant

Romans 15:1–7

'Accept one another, then, just as Christ accepted you' (v7)

C an a friendship survive if just one person is tolerant? Do both parties need to be tolerant if it's to flourish? Some of us are patient by nature; for others it can take a great deal of effort! Let's take a pen and paper, then list *how* and *why* St Paul says we should be 'enduring' (see verse 5).

Here are some other 'one another' verses which are helpful in this respect:

'Live in harmony with one another. Do not be proud' (Rom. 12:16); 'let us stop passing judgment on one another' (Rom. 14:13); 'Let us not become conceited, provoking and envying each other' (Gal. 5:26).

If we can keep our thoughts and attitudes in check, then it will help us to rein in our negative reactions. Then our conversation will not deteriorate. 'If you bite and devour each other, watch out or you will be destroyed by each other' (Gal. 5:15). That's a strong warning.

As I've said previously, the heart of the 'one another' verses is 'love' – and the way to express this is via forgiveness. So let us determine to forgive our friends with the forgiveness which Christ has lavished upon us.

Optional further reading

Colossians 3:12–17

Thomas Jones and Steve Brown, *One Another: Transformational Relationships in the Body of Christ* (Spring Hill, TN: DPI Books, 2008)

Forgiveness

Matthew 18:21–35

'Lord, how many times shall I forgive my brother or sister…?' (v21)

O ne of my poems* begins like this:

> 'That word – it hurt so much. It was cruel and unjust, Uncaring.
> That word – still causes pain. It has gone very deep, Pervading.
> That word – troubles my mind. It goes round in my thoughts, Provoking.'

Jesus' story describes heartless actions. My poem acknowledges unkind words. I'm sure we can identify with both! But when I'm hurt by a friend, experience has taught me that I need to keep my emotions in check and remember that I'm none too perfect either! Instead of stewing on their failure to apologise, I have to deliberately choose to 'take captive every thought' as advised by St Paul (2 Cor. 10:5). It's hard not to dwell on blame, but God's way is to bring restoration (as Jesus demonstrated by resolving the issue of our redemption at the cross).

In my favourite classic novel, *Jane Eyre* by Charlotte Bronte, Jane lived a desolate, isolated existence appearing to have few friends. However, during her time at Lowood School, fellow pupil Helen Burns was there to show her the path to Christian forgiveness. Do you have a friend who could offer you counsel if necessary? And would you be prepared to become vulnerable in the process?

If we make the effort to forgive, it's in our own best interest. Matthew 6:15 puts it bluntly: 'if you do not forgive others their sins, your Father will not forgive your sins'. And reconciliation with a fellow human being will reduce our inner turmoil, improve our mental health and can help prevent similar issues arising within our friendships in the future.

*Rachel Hall-Smith, *That Word!*

For prayer and reflection

Father, I choose to forgive as You have forgiven me. In times of disagreement, grant me wisdom and Your peace. Amen.

Betrayal

**Matthew
26:14–16,36–50**

'Jesus replied, "Do
what you came for,
friend."' (v50)

Being hurt or saddened by a confidant is not the same as being betrayed by them. Prior to this incident in the Garden of Gethsemane, 'many of [Jesus'] disciples turned back and no longer followed him' (John 6:66), but never before had He been let down on this scale. Receiving a kiss from one of His inner circle, Jesus was earmarked for physical cruelty, ridicule and an excruciating death.

This was a unique situation but we cannot understate the pain any person might experience if they're double-crossed or deserted. Let's turn to Psalm 55:12–21 and read David's story.

It's particularly sad that David's distress was caused not only by a friend but by a fellow believer (v14). Let's be honest – we have higher expectations of people within church walls and therefore the offence seems greater. And are we, like David, tempted to run away from the conflict to escape the pain? 'Oh, that I had the wings of a dove!... I would hurry to my place of shelter, far from the tempest and storm' (vv6,8). However, David concludes by giving himself and those who have faced such misery subsequently, some timely advice: 'Cast your cares on the LORD and he will sustain you' (v22). We know this to be true, as Jesus faced and conquered rejection and punishment beyond belief.

Sadly, Judas felt unable to believe that there was any hope of him being reconciled to Jesus, and it seems the same was true of David and his former 'friend' described in Psalm 55. It's sometimes hard to accept, but differences do occur. If this is something that you have experienced, cling to the truth that whilst friends can be faithless, God is totally trustworthy.

**For prayer
and reflection**

**Reflect on
Romans 12:14:
'Bless those who
persecute you;
bless and do
not curse.'**

Friends with a **mission**

Today we read of friends with a common purpose – to see Jesus glorified. Their 'quest' was to see others won to Christ. As I've stated before, many of my best friends are Christians. Jesus is the centre of my universe, so it's natural for me to gravitate towards others who feel the same.

At my church, we attempt to bless other ladies and share our faith by organising afternoon teas, baby showers and similar events. It's a contemporary way of following in the footsteps of these New Testament women. But what about friends who're unwilling to enter the doors of our church? Verse 5 is most encouraging in this respect, as it speaks of the first conversion in a new locality. So, as we build relationships in our community, we earn respect and the opportunity to share our faith.

How can we foster friendships with people who don't yet know Jesus if all our activities are church-centred? Responsibilities can limit opportunities in the workplace, so a positive step is to proactively participate in social groups (sports clubs – or choirs, writing groups etc for the less active amongst us). Which pastimes 'beyond church walls' could you use as a mission field? And what inventive ways can you come up with to welcome friends into church activities?

Our friendship can often speak louder than words, but it's good to remind ourselves to be *on the lookout* for circumstances in which it's timely to share our faith. Some of us will find this easier to do than others! It's tempting to hesitate, as we don't wish to offend or to spoil our relationship. So, let's pray for boldness and good opportunities!

Romans 16:1–16

'Greet Tryphena and Tryphosa, those women who work hard in the Lord' (v12)

For prayer and reflection

Lord, I pray that Your Spirit will prepare the way for me to have a positive spiritual influence on my friends. Amen.

Division

Acts 15:36–41

'They had such a sharp disagreement that they parted company.' (v39)

By now, you'll have realised that I'm not going into much detail regarding my own friendships, and I've done this deliberately to preserve personal confidences. I've known my dearest friends for a long time, although I had the joy of making a new friend last year and we've immediately become close. But I'm sad to say that on one occasion in my lifetime, a friend and I 'deliberately lost touch'.

Paul and Barnabas were friends who served the Lord in partnership. They taught together and had a mighty impact as joint apostles to the churches (14:1,15). But... things went wrong.

And this wasn't an isolated dispute between Jesus' followers. His disciples had disagreed between themselves (see Matt. 20:24) and Martha became understandably frustrated with Mary for slacking. As she prepared food for Jesus and His disciples, she grumbled 'Lord, don't you care that my sister has left me to do the work by myself? Tell her to help me!' (Luke 10:40). I can hear the anger in her complaint but, interestingly, Jesus shared Mary's perspective. Even as Christians, with the very best intentions, we will sometimes get things wrong.

When differences do occur, we need to judge how best to handle them. To never lose sight of our precious common goal – to see people find a relationship with Jesus – is paramount. I believe that's why Paul and Barnabas decided to part company. God's purpose needed to be put above all lesser disagreement. And if they hadn't decided to go their separate ways, trouble may have filtered into the wider church.

We can always hope and aim to resolve our differences, but sometimes we can only agree to disagree.

For prayer and reflection

Reflect on Romans 12:18: 'If it is possible, as far as it depends on you, live at peace with everyone.'

Prayer

Daniel 2:14–23

'He urged them to plead for mercy from the God of heaven concerning this mystery' (v18)

D o you pray for your friends? And if so, what do you pray about? While experiencing some family difficulties recently, I sent regular texts to a couple of close friends to update them on our prayer needs. Daniel does the equivalent of this in today's reading. These friends would empathise with him as they'd already been through so much together. They'd been exiled and ended up serving a foreign king who had high expectations. But this tricky situation was about to become a lot more heated! (You can read about the 'blazing furnace' incident in the next chapter.)

For many it is natural to pray for those who are facing life and death situations, but St Paul prayed for his friends *continuously* and with *thanksgiving*, whatever their circumstances (1 Thess. 1:2). This conveyed his genuine care and love for them. In return, he urged them to reciprocate: 'Devote yourselves to prayer, being watchful and thankful. And pray for us, too, that God may open a door for our message' (Col. 4:2–3). Paul understood that prayer makes a huge difference.

It's such a privilege to be able to carry *everything* to the Lord in prayer. Sometimes the needs are obvious and we can cry with those who are heartbroken and celebrate with those who delight. But when circumstances are not so clear cut, the Spirit is there to guide our intercession. (Please read Rom. 8:26–27.) And, as we pray for our friends (and our future friends?), we can be assured that we're following in the footsteps of Jesus too: 'My prayer is not that you take them out of the world but that you protect them from the evil one' (John 17:15).

For prayer and reflection

Pray on behalf of each of your close friends today.

Be supportive

....

1 Peter 4:8–11

'serve others, as faithful stewards of God's grace' (v10)

Part of being 'devoted to one another' (Rom. 12:10) is to be supportive *emotionally*, as we've seen in the lives of Elizabeth, Mary and other biblical characters. Of particular relevance are the verses: 'Carry each other's burdens' (Gal. 6:2); and 'encourage one another and build each other up' (1 Thess. 5:11).

Today, however, I want to focus on being *practically* supportive. Whatever our abilities, we're urged to use them for the benefit of others, to draw on God's enabling and to do it for His glory. We have previously read the following verses, but this weekend I'd encourage us to mediate on Galatians 5:13 and make Romans 12:13 a matter for prayer:

'You... were called to be free. But do not use your freedom to indulge the flesh; rather, serve one another humbly in love' (Gal. 5:13). 'Share with the Lord's people who are in need. Practise hospitality' (Rom. 12:13).

Let's commit to making ourselves available to our friends, being alert to their needs, maybe offering practical help or initiating prayer support.

....

Optional further reading

John 13:1–17; 15:1–8

Life givers

2 Timothy
1:1–14

'What you heard
from me, keep as
the pattern of
sound teaching'
(v13)

I think it's wonderful that 'Inspiring Women' goes so much further than these notes. I recently attended a Woman to Woman course at Waverley Abbey House. Rosalyn Derges, one of the leaders, commented on the value of friends whom she describes as 'spark people' – those who encourage you rather than pull you down. Lynette coined the phrase 'life givers'. Timothy was positively influenced by both his gran and mum (v5) but his friend Paul still took the trouble to write to him, in order to build his faith and confidence to minister.

Reread verses 9, 12 and 14 of today's reading and identify the wisdom that Paul dispensed. These are great snippets of advice that we can share within our friendship groups, however young we consider ourselves to be in the faith. But often it's our behaviour, habits and spiritual discipline which are noticed alongside our speech. A challenging thought.

Paul isn't the only biblical character who chose to mentor someone less mature in faith. Elijah shared between six and ten years with Elisha (biblical historians disagree on the precise timescale) and from their first meeting, Elisha was being prepared to be his successor. In 2 Kings 2, we see Elisha observing and then replicating Elijah's behaviour: 'When he struck the water, it divided to the right and to the left, and he crossed over' (v14).

It's invaluable when mature Christian women befriend younger Christian women. The relationship doesn't have to be 'one way'! While Elijah's motivation was to mentor, Elisha provided *him* with much needed support. Who can you draw alongside today to mentor? Who might be a mentor to you?

For prayer and reflection

Father, may Your Holy Spirit inspire and equip me to encourage and build up my friends in their faith. Amen.

Honesty

**Ephesians
4:1–16**

'speaking the truth
in love, we will
grow' (v15)

I n my Christian friendships, am I more likely to be the one in need, or the one offering support? (I may have to take some time to think about this!) Take a moment to re-read verse 16, as it not only summarises the whole passage but suggests how, ideally, Christian friends should relate.

Our key verse leads us to consider a number of further questions: Do I have a friend who'd feel able to challenge me if the need were to arise? Would I feel affronted or be humble enough to consider whether my friend had a point? Would I have the right attitude (vv2–3) and confidence to do the same for my friend? Our answers will depend on whether we have a friend whom we've learned to trust deeply, and whose discernment and spiritual maturity we value.

It takes courage to have a friendship at this level. But listen to these words from Proverbs: 'Wounds from a friend can be trusted' (27:6). The book of James takes things a step further: 'confess your sins to each other and pray for each other so that you may be healed' (5:16). So if we're bold enough to be truthful, a loving friend's prayer support can lead to spiritual progress and wholeness.

I've noticed that the importance of prayer has threaded itself seamlessly though our readings this month, and it's imperative here. If we're wishing to speak tactfully to a friend, we need to pray for guidance, timing, a dose of love and that they'll listen with God's help. Being honest about our own foibles and weaknesses (and the fact that we're not always right) is important. And never breaking a confidence is essential. They may well return the favour on a different occasion!

**For prayer
and reflection**

**Father, help
me to develop
friendships which
have depth,
openness and
honesty, so that
we can be of
mutual support
during testing
times. Amen.**

Friendships are **priceless**

Ecclesiastes 4:9–12

'A cord of three strands is not quickly broken.' (v12)

You may wonder why I'm ending with a reading from Ecclesiastes, given that chapter one starts with the assertion 'Everything is meaningless'! However, after making observations on life, the writer concludes that without God life is bleak. I'd agree with that. And I also think that a life without friends would be very bleak indeed. In the words of W.B. Yeats: 'Think where man's glory most begins and ends, and say my glory was I had such friends.'

God injects joy into every area of our lives, including our friendships. And if two human friends link with Him, a rope made of three strands is hard to break. Each of us can be more productive (v9), a help in time of need (v10) and provide great comfort.

We read in Exodus that God called Moses to lead the Israelites from captivity in Egypt (3:7–10). Yet Moses felt inadequate. So his brother Aaron became his speaker and supporter (Exod. 4:10–16). This friendship enhanced Moses' ministry and enabled a nation's escape from Egypt.

Without friends, life can feel empty. If you need evidence of this, please read verse 8, which precedes today's reading. Is there anyone whom you'd like to get to know better? If so, what could you do to help this process in the light of our reflections this month?

Proverbs 27:17 states that 'As iron sharpens iron, so one person sharpens another'. Yet another strange analogy. (One minute relationships are compared to old rope and then they're associated with metal treated in a foundry!) But it's true. Significant friendships are mutually strengthening and can hone our lives. And besides... we can have great fun in the process!

For prayer and reflection

Thank You, Lord, for the friends I so value. God bless each of them and those who will be special to me in the future. Amen.

Judy Moore

Judy Moore is part of the leadership team at Riverside Church, Birmingham, and is also a freelancer actor and writer. She talks to us about the power of storytelling...

This is what I've decided my life statement is: *I will be woman of a free and light spirit, extending the table of celebration, living and telling the story of Jesus Christ and excelling in love.* 'Fine words,' I hear you cry, 'but does she live up to them?' The short answer is of course no – but this is what I'm aiming for! Living and telling the story of Jesus is what I believe I'm put on this earth to do. I'm a storyteller at heart and have always loved to act, speak and write to that end. I also believe that humour

is vital to the Christian life and was a huge part of Jesus' communication and the stories He told.

My ten-year-old self wanted to be an actress, was worryingly obsessed with prisons, and did not enjoy church. So if you'd told that same girl that she was to become a church leader, she would most definitely have laughed loudly (though apparently I did used to preach to my toys, so maybe there was something there all along).

Growing up, I didn't believe I was 'churchy' enough; I wasn't naturally instinctively 'good', and didn't like to play by the rules. I counted myself out of faith and church at the age of 13, but at the age of 19, while acting in a soap opera for a beach mission, I was completely floored by the love, forgiveness and healing of Jesus.

Since then, having worked for over ten years for Saltmine Theatre Company and now working as a freelancer with Searchlight theatre company, my childhood dream of acting has found fulfilment – but so has my latent obsession with prisons (which perhaps birthed when I was five, regularly driving past Dartmoor prison). We have put on plays, led workshops and prayed with many adult prisoners to find hope and forgiveness in Jesus. One young man had been told that he was a mistake and had lived his whole life believing it. When we read Psalm 139, about his whole life being part of God's plan, he became really angry, accusing us of spreading lies. As we prayed together and told him of our total confidence that his life was definitely meant to be, and that he had even been used by God to bless us that very week, he was overwhelmed. He asked for a copy of 'that poem, Miss,' to put on his wall. I was moved to tears by the Bible's power to speak into all our stories, reversing the lies we have believed.

I've often been asked about my journey from acting to church leadership, but for me there are many parallels. For both pastor and actor, the aim is to get the 'audience' to listen and understand their message; their heart. I long to help people discover the very best version of themselves in Jesus, and to explore the good works God has prepared in advance for all of us to do (Eph. 2:10).

I've been told that in my writing, leadership and speaking, there is a 'fragility'. When I began speaking regularly, a lovely friend gave me a tea light holder covered in handmade paper, and told me that where the paper was most delicate was where the light would shine brightest. He said that mine would be a ministry where Christ's love would shine and, in my weaknesses and wounded places, He would shine even brighter.

I truly believe that God has dreams for us to live out, dissatisfactions for us to address, people for us to love and celebrate, and – perhaps best of all – some wonderful opportunities to laugh along the way!

Judy is the author of *The Dog Who Thought His Name Was No* (CWR, 2017), and *The Bird Who Lost Its Song* (to be published early next year).

A Resilient Life

DIANE REGAN

Romans 3:21–24

'and all are justified freely by his grace through the redemption that came by Christ Jesus.' (v24)

Every person, since time began, is completely unique. Not only do we each have our own thumb print and DNA, we all have our own stories; our own journeys. Our lives are made up of our life experiences – the bad as well as the good, the failures as well as the successes.

One of the most comforting things I have learned is that making mistakes is OK. It does not mean we are failures; it means we are human. No matter who we are, where we are from, our age or our education, we will let people down and we will get things wrong – probably even on a daily basis. The Bible is filled with stories of people who messed up, made mistakes and got things wrong. At the same time, however, through God's love and grace, so many of these characters are also celebrated for their good works and deeds, their obedience and most importantly their faith.

We can be extremely grateful that God does not look for our record of successes before He pours out His love for us or chooses to use us. He delights and specialises in turning what the world throws out as waste, into redeemed hope and a positive future. Our loving Father wastes nothing. He wants us to grow and thrive. Despite our past, despite our failures, our wrong choices, our mistakes, His grace is freely available for all of us, releasing us and bringing freedom and hope. It is so freeing to know that we don't need to live perfect lives. All we need to do is bring who we are honestly before God. He does not *have* to use us, but he chooses to. What an absolute privilege.

For prayer and reflection

Lord, thank You for Your totally undeserved grace. Help me to understand more the reality of Your love and hope. Amen.

Resting in the storm

Many biggest conclusion about life is this: it's hard, but it's so much harder without God. I honestly do not know how people navigate the journey of life without our heavenly Father. There are so many decisions we have to make, and it can be overwhelming – particularly when we have the freedom to make significant and potentially life-changing decisions. We cannot see the future, but we do have an open invitation for a living relationship with the Most High, the Almighty one, who is the beginning and the end. God's patient and loving guidance is available to us every single day.

Two key words in verse 1 are 'dwell' and 'rest'. In order to achieve the rest, we need first to dwell. To dwell requires time. It is not a quick visit or a flick through the Bible. It is an intentional effort to spend time and consciously remain with Jesus. That doesn't have to mean hiding away in a prayer closet, it means taking Jesus with us through our day – including our decisions. With this comes the 'rest'. Knowing we are not on our own. Having confidence that the Almighty is watching over us and is with us. The closer we are to Him, the more we can lean in and rest in Him.

Psalm 91 depicts a raging storm, and we know that life can feel this way at times. But we read about the Lord covering us with His wings, rescuing and protecting, and bringing deliverance and salvation. When in the midst of a storm, it can be difficult to remember that God is there, let alone be in a state of rest. The miracle is that God *is* still with us, fighting our battles with us, regardless of whether we feel it or not.

Psalm 91:1–16

'Whoever dwells in the shelter of the Most High will rest in the shadow of the Almighty.' (v1)

For prayer and reflection

Lord, thank You that Your Word promises You are always with me, providing shelter, even in the storms. Help me to remember this and learn to dwell and find rest. Amen.

Weekend

He is in the waiting

....

Psalm 27:7–14

'Wait for the LORD; be strong and take heart and wait for the LORD.' (v14)

I remember going forward for prayer in response to a call to those wanting to give their lives to God's service. I remember having felt frustrated at my lack of service up to that point. The lady praying was so patient and filled with wisdom, and after a few minutes of praying, she had a picture of a horse and cart. Just as a cart attached to a horse, following where the horse leads, this was to be my role. I needed to stop pushing ahead, taking on the role of the horse. That role belongs to Jesus. My role was to stay close, following His lead. This was such a simple picture, yet it made a lot of sense to me.

There have since been many times when it has felt as if the horse is not going anywhere, and I have had to wait. This has been especially hard when I have had a hope or expectation of where the horse might be going. The temptation to push ahead is often difficult. However, He is in the waiting. I am forced to rest, prepare, tune in and focus on the horse, not the destination. As I do this, the destination ceases to be so important, and often it is at this point that we start moving again.

....

Optional further reading

Laurie Short, *Finding Faith in the Dark* (Grand Rapids, MI, USA: Zondervan, 2014)

Noticing the little things

'Indeed, the very hairs of your head are all numbered.' (v7)

W e often have meetings in our home, and inevitably at some point, we're asked where the loo is. On one occasion, someone visited the loo, came back to the lounge, picked up her phone and returned to the loo. She eventually explained how she found our loo inspiring and wanted to take a picture of the beautifully decorated quote we had on the wall, by the American writer Kurt Vonnegut: 'Enjoy the little things in life, for one day you will look back and realise they are the big things.' We spent some time talking about how significant the quote was for her, because she was facing some big challenges.

Naturally, it is easier to notice the big things. Whether good or bad, the big things can take priority. The tallest person, the top achieving children, the most expensive car, the biggest house. On the contrary, God is interested in *all* things, big and small. Think about the intricate detail He put into designing the beautiful ladybird; the amazing strength and ability He gave to the tiny ants. He even knows how many hairs we have on our head.

Taking time to notice and appreciate the little things helps us to cope with the big things, particularly when life becomes overwhelming. Focusing on a smile from a stranger passing by, a wildflower on the side of the road, the laugh of a toddler playing, your favourite song playing on the radio – noticing these things can help fill our emotional tanks. It is so easy to pass them by. They could be seen as trivial or coincidences. Or they could be appreciated as little drops of heaven, sent by God to help you get through your day.

For prayer and reflection

I am grateful, Lord, that You see me. You know everything about me, my needs, hopes and disappointments. You know what I need for today and I choose to trust You. Amen.

Looking at the wrong thing

**Matthew
6:25–34**

'But seek first his
kingdom and his
righteousness' (v33)

As I was out walking the dogs recently, I knew I had to navigate a narrow path through stinging nettles. I was so pleased that I had avoided getting stung as I entered the final meadow that I took my eyes off the path. Ouch. I was caught by the tiniest, single nettle. Probably the only one in the meadow. Isn't there a parallel here for life? How many times have I been working hard to navigate through a tricky period in my life, when the most unexpected thing comes along and takes me by surprise? It could be a small thing like a nettle, or it could be something big.

Also very recently, I had a tight deadline to meet and was annoyed that my son hadn't managed to arrange a lift home from football practice. I pulled out of my drive and didn't see the car parked on the side of the road. Bang. I had no excuse. I was looking at the wrong thing.

So how do we make sure we're looking at the right thing? What *is* the right thing? The good news is, it's not about what we physically look at; it's about the attitude of our heart – what we seek.

**For prayer
and reflection**

Dear Lord, thank You that You are always with me and that You want the best for me, despite how things may appear. Help me to see things as You see them. Amen.

Despite these two negative situations, seeing things through God's kingdom eyes changed things. I am now more careful on my walks and have started to notice more of God's creation, and I have changed my diary so that I collect my son and spend that weekly time with him.

Mistakes and accidents do happen. On both of these occasions, I was extremely grateful for sting relief cream, forgiving car owners (and husbands) and insurance companies. God does not always stop bad things from happening, but that doesn't mean He isn't there, going through them with us.

Just **one** thing

Psalm 27:1–6

'One thing I ask from the LORD… that I may dwell in the house of the LORD all the days of my life' (v4)

We were running an icebreaker activity and asked the question, 'If you were stranded on an island and could have any three things, what would they be?' The group found answering this harder than they expected, but then eventually came up with the ideas of: a fishing rod, a knife and a solar-powered mobile phone (with signal). When pushed to then reduce items down to just one thing, they wanted - yes, you guessed it – the mobile phone.

We are built for connection; it is wired into us as part of our DNA. God designed us this way. David wrote in today's psalm that the one thing he asked for was to be able to dwell with God every day. David desired fellowship and communion with God. Back then, to meet with God, or to be able to 'dwell', you had to physically go to the Tabernacle. This required effort, time and dedication.

Even in Jesus' time, you had to go to the Temple to be with God. Jesus' death and resurrection and the promise of the Holy Spirit means this is no longer a requirement. If we ask Him to, God has promised He will be with us all the time.

For the majority of people, mobile phones are important possessions as they connect us to everything. We are tempted to have them with us constantly, often for very valid reasons.

David lived and wrote the Psalms about 1,000 BC, before any technology was ever invented, yet His words still resonate with us today. If dwelling with God all the days of our lives was the one thing we focused on and desired, how different would we be today? How would this change our priorities, fears, plans and hopes?

For prayer and reflection

Spend a moment considering what your focus is on today. What does your heart dwell on?

Going **God's** way

Proverbs 3:1–6

'Trust in the LORD with all your heart and lean not on your own understanding' (v5)

When I was new to faith, everything seemed so obvious and clear: God was the hero who was able to fix anything, and there were mostly happy endings. If it was not a happy ending, there was always a reason to blame things on. As the years and their experiences have gone on, there is now more in my life that I do not understand, and even more that I realise I do not know.

As a new Christian, I expected to need God less as I learned and matured. In reality, however, the opposite is true. As each day passes, I am more reliant on God than ever. I need Him more and more every day.

The plan I had for my life came and went many years ago. I am sure this is true for most people! Looking back, I can see how, although God has been constantly with me and I am amazed at how although He does not cause bad things to happen, He uses these times for good. My pain and scars of the past can now help others. God has used my journey to change me, to enable me to listen more, to build my resilience and to soften me up. I have learned that it is not about me, my desires and my dreams (although these are important, and most often God-given). God's plans are far greater than my dreams and desires.

It is not about how clever we are, how much we have in the bank, how big our house, how fast our car. Mother Theresa had nothing, no qualifications or official status, yet ended up being one of the most influential people ever to live. Her simple message was to love without judgment and to find beauty in everyone. Her simple acts of love and kindness have left lasting impact on the world.

For prayer and reflection

Lord, Your ways are perfect. You are the beginning and the end. Thank You that even though I am just one person in the whole universe, You still choose to use me. Amen.

Undeserved good and bad

James 1:16–18

How often do you hear people, particularly children, say the words 'It's not fair'? Having four children of my own, I have heard it many times. And it's true, life is not fair. Test results do come back with devastating news, marriages do break up, loved ones do pass away, accidents do happen, employees do lose jobs. Many times, it's not fair; it's undeserved.

'Every good and perfect gift is from above, coming down from the Father' (v17)

So what do we deserve? How should it work? Should the positive things that happen in our lives be according to how good we are, how hard we work?

It's helpful here to consider the undeserved *good* in our lives. Have we had people to love and people who have loved us? Do we have a place to sleep? Do we have enough food for the next meal? Do we have the opportunity to see the sunrise or the sunset? Have we people around us who could help us in time of need? Someone we can call on for prayer? These may be simple things, but they are gifts. I am certain there is so much more in each day you could add to your list of undeserved good.

When I was first taught about the word 'grace', I was given the acronym 'God's Riches At Christ's Expense'. This centres me and reminds me about what Jesus went through on my behalf. His death was the ultimate example of unfairness. So, yes, the undeserved bad happens, and it can often feel as if there is more bad than good, but Jeremiah 17:7 promises, 'blessed is the one who trusts in the LORD'. When we take time to look at our blessings now and in days gone by, we can be filled with joy, knowing that regardless of who we are or what we've done, our loving Father showers us with good and perfect gifts from above.

For prayer and reflection

Father, thank You for the undeserved provision You bless me with every day. Please open my eyes to see more of Your wonderful work in my life. Amen.

Stronger than each storm

. . . .

Acts 27:13–25

'keep up your courage… for I have faith in God' (v25)

Today's passage depicts Paul in a boat going through a storm. We're told how the storm was so violent the people on board 'finally gave up all hope of being saved' (v20). They had thrown all excess cargo overboard in order to help keep the boat afloat, meaning that on top of the fear and loss of hope, they were hungry. After many days, at the point of no hope, Paul had a vision of an angel in the night and was told the boat would be destroyed but not one life would be lost. Reading to the end of the chapter, we find out there were 276 people on board. The account is amazing.

A few years ago, my husband and I felt as if we were in a tiny boat being tossed around by huge waves in the middle of an unknown ocean. We had no idea where we were going; we could not see any direction, either by daylight or stars during the night. We did not even have faith we would safely reach a shore. During this time, we found comfort in the prayer of Saint Brendan: 'I trust You to be stronger than each storm within me. I will trust in the darkness and know that my times, even now, are in Your hand.' Amen to that.

. . . .

Optional further reading

Patrick Regan, *Honesty Over Silence* (Farnham: CWR, 2018)

Muscle growth

1 Timothy 4:4–8

'For physical training is of some value, but godliness has value for all things' (v8)

Imagine resilience is like a muscle. Firstly, in order for the muscle to grow, it has to break a little. Body builders increase their muscle capacity by exercising, pushing themselves further, lifting heavier and heavier weights. Athletes exercise in a similar way: pushing themselves to run further and faster. It hurts, but this intentional pain increases their ability. The breakage in the fibres of the muscles causes the body to repair the muscle and therefore make it stronger.

In the same way, going through difficult and challenging times in our lives, when we feel broken, has the ability to make us stronger.

Secondly, it is important to note that rest plays a huge role in building up the muscle, in repairing the broken fibres. If the muscle does not have the opportunity to rest, it will not repair and get stronger – it will remain broken. This is also true for resilience.

When we go through a difficult time or when we're in survival mode, we can only continue for so long. We need to recognise when to stop and rest, allowing ourselves to repair and strengthen in order continue. Taking time out can be difficult, but it is vital.

The third thing a muscle needs in order to grow is the right nutrition. Comparing this to ourselves and resilience, healthy eating does of course help, but we also need to healthily feed our mind, spirit and soul. There is little point in exercising and resting well if we then fill ourselves with the wrong things. Today's passage encourages us to live healthily in our spirit and soul too through thanksgiving, and through prayer. What do you think that might look like for you today?

For prayer and reflection

Lord, You have the best food for my mind, spirit and soul. Thank You that I can come to You to refresh and rebuild strength into my life. Amen.

Bouncing back

Ephesians 2:4–10

'For we are God's handiwork… to do good works, which God prepared in advance for us to do.' (v10)

I love the fictional character Tigger who features in a lot of *Winnie the Pooh* stories by A.A. Milne. In the illustrations by Ernest H. Shepard that accompany the stories, Tigger has an exceptionally strong and long tail that he coils like a spring and uses to bounce. He has a wonderfully positive personality, and is always wanting to help and get involved, despite often becoming more of a hindrance than a help. Regardless of how disastrous his contribution may end up being, Tigger always manages to bounce back in a positive way. He is often quoted, 'Life is not about how fast you run or how high you climb but how well you bounce.' On this occasion, I could not agree more with Tigger.

Resilience is often described as bouncing back. But without a long and strong tail, coiled like a spring, how do we do this?

One of the key ways Tigger was able to 'bounce' was by being confident in using his natural gifts and talents. He is famously known for not being able to climb trees, and once he knew this was not his gifting, he was OK with it and stopped trying.

Have we spent time working out what God has prepared in advance for us to do, or are we trying to a job we are not called to do, which requires talents and giftings God has not given us? Let's consider what natural talents and giftings God *has* given us that will help us to bounce through life. These abilities are His handiwork, personally designed for us. They are our unique tools. Using them hand in hand with God can lead to an exciting adventure. The most important thing is to listen to Him and follow His lead.

For prayer and reflection

Spend time considering your God-given gifts. If you are not sure of them, start by listing what you enjoy, what you are good at and what others say you are good at.

Grit

Hebrews 12:1–3

'And let us run with
perseverance the
race marked out
for us' (v1)

Angela Duckworth is a contemporary American academic and psychologist who coined the term 'grit' in her study of what enables success. Angela describes grit as 'perseverance and passion for long-term goals', which leads to success.*

Yesterday we looked at talents, abilities and giftings, and spent some time considering what our God-given gifts are. Today we are looking at the role of goals in resilience. If we know what we are living for, what we are using our gifts and abilities for, then this helps us to be able to keep going through life's rollercoaster ups and downs.

The pilot of a plane will know the landing destination. However, rarely will the plane's journey be a direct, straight line from the starting point to the landing point. The pilot has to navigate the plane through a whole host of situations, such as other planes in the sky, wind thermals and varied weather conditions.

In the same way, knowing our long-term goal does not mean we can plan our route exactly, but it does give us an idea of the direction we need to go in. We need to be flexible to allow for the ups and downs. Life happens, we will make mistakes and we will face challenges along the way, but having our end goal helps to get back up and keep going.

As Christians, our overall long-term goal is to worship Jesus and to be a conduit for others to know Him. This requires perseverance and, certainly, passion. Our level of focus on this goal determines our level of grit, and impacts every area of our lives. It's good to know that Jesus is with us every step of the way.

*To read more, search online for Angela Duckworth's article, 'Grit: Perseverance and passion for long-term goals'.

For prayer and reflection

Spend some time considering your long-term goals in life. Are they realistic and achievable? Do they need refining?

Capability

1 Peter 5:6–10

'And the God of all grace… will himself restore you and make you strong, firm and steadfast.' (v10)

According to the Royal College of Psychiatrists, we need the following five things to cope well in life: to accept ourselves and know what we need; to have caring relationships with people; to have clear expectations of ourselves and others; to be part of a community; and to be believed in.

As Christians, we could rewrite this as: to be honest, vulnerable and courageous; to love and be loved in a supportive environment; to live in accordance with God's Word; to be in communion with God, and in fellowship with other Christians; to be accepted and valued.

God's plan is not just for us to cope, but to flourish. We cannot do this on our own, and as Christians it is comforting to know we are not on our own.

We need to be honest, vulnerable and courageous. For some of us this means removing our mask. For some of us it means accepting where we are and asking for help. Being part of God's family can bring huge blessing. It is wonderful that in God's kingdom there is no barrier of race, age, culture or background. We also need to spend time reading God's word and in prayer. Through this, we will know more of the life-changing truth that we are accepted, loved and valued by our loving Father just as we are.

Take a moment to think about your own life and prayerfully consider those two lists of things we need in order to cope well in life – the list suggested by psychiatrists, and the suggested list for us as Christians. Although we know we have a loving God who is with us all the time, is He nudging you to work on an area in your life at the moment? Are you spending time with Him, with others, and accepting yourself? While it's true that these things require vulnerability, they allow us to flourish.

For prayer and reflection

Thank You, Father, that I am not on my own, that You love me completely and that You want me to not just cope but flourish and be all You have made me to be. Amen.

Waverley Abbey College

'We are all on a journey of discovery when it comes to the matters of the soul, and it is always good to question what we are saying and doing in relation to helping people and their problems.' – Selwyn Hughes, Founder of CWR

Our programmes equip students with the skills and knowledge to release their God-given potential to operate in roles that help people.

Central to all of our teaching is the Waverley Integrative Framework. Built on 50 years of experience, the model emphasises the importance of genuineness, unconditional acceptance and empathy in relationships.

Counselling

As society begins to realise the extent of its brokenness, we continue to recognise the need to train people to support those who are struggling with everyday life, providing training to equip individuals to become professional counsellors. Whatever their starting point in academic learning, we have a pathway to help all students on their academic journey.

Spiritual Formation

For those wanting to be better equipped to help others on their spiritual journey, this programme provides robust and effective Spiritual Formation training. Students engage with theology, psychology, social sciences, historical studies, counselling, leadership studies and psychotherapy.

For more information about all of our course offerings available, visit **waverleyabbeycollege.ac.uk** or come along to a free Open Day.

Antifragile

**Colossians
1:15–20**

'He is before all
things, and in him
all things hold
together.' (v17)

The opposite of resilience is fragility. Nassim Nichoals Taleb, a scholar and former trader and risk analyst, came up with the term 'antifragile' following his work focusing on problems of randomness, probability and uncertainty. He then wrote his book, *Antifragile: Things that Gain from Disorder*. According to Taleb, antifragility is beyond resilience or robustness. The resilient resists or deals with issues but may stay the same; the antifragile focus on the learning that can result of an issue and uses the experience to improve.

The airline industry is a good example of antifragile – every time there is an incident, they open up to other airlines and share all the technical details of what they understand to have happened so that everyone is stronger in the long run. That way, other aircrafts can fix any potential faults. It's why there are incredibly low numbers of incidents on passenger aircraft, despite millions of flights every year.

Practicing antifragility therefore requires honesty and vulnerability – being honest with ourselves and showing vulnerability to others – which is not easy.

The title for today's reading in the NIV is, 'The supremacy of the Son of God'. Jesus is the supreme example of antifragile. He is beyond resilience, outside of time and space. Jesus is beyond perfection. Taleb looked at the benefit drawn out of chaos, and created a new word, yet God was already there before time began. He brought order and beauty out of nothing and created the whole world. What a privilege to be part of His family, that we can call Him Father. In our efforts to become antifragile, let's look to the invincible Jesus.

**For prayer
and reflection**

**Father, You
created the whole
universe, yet You
call me daughter.
There is nothing in
my life that is too
big or too difficult
for me to come to
You with. Amen.**

Different types of resilience

Psalm 46:8–11

'Be still and know that I am God' (v10)

There are many different types of resilience: engineering resilience – improving a product to be stronger; plant resilience – developing to withstand the environment (such as deeper roots in windier places); psychological resilience – the capacity to recover quickly.

This last type, psychological resilience can be broken down even more. A quick Google search can include the following catgories: social, family, community, organisational, cultural, emotional, mental etc.

The three main words from the above list are 'improving', 'developing' and 'recover'. These are all active words, so why do we have in the key verse the instruction to 'be still'? These two words alone are the opposite of action. However, the additional words, 'and know that I am God' are an active challenge that requires knowledge, faith and trust – and these take time to build. This active command requires our commitment to improve, to develop and helps us to recover. Verse 10 is close to the end of a whole psalm about how God is our refuge and strength. As a Christian, understanding what it means to be a daughter of the Almighty can help us live with resilience.

Optional further reading

Tom and Christine Sine, *Living on Purpose* (Grand Rapids, MI, USA: Baker Books, 2002)

A life with **meaning**

Acts 2:42–47

'They devoted
themselves to the
apostles' teaching
and to fellowship'
(v42)

Since the turn of the century, there has been a lot of research into resilience. Until this point, it was generally accepted that it was all to do with genetics: some people were just naturally able to cope with life better than others, although there were useful skills that could be learned to help improve their ability to cope. As part of a recent study, research was carried out to determine if there were common characteristics among those who survived concentration camps, and over the next few days we will take a look at the findings.

The common characteristic was a sense of meaning for their lives. Victor Frankl was a holocaust survivor. During his time in the camp he developed 'meaning therapy', which is explained in his book *Man's Search for Meaning*. For Frankl, meaning came from having purposeful work, love and courage in the face of difficulty.

The most resilient establishment in the world to date is the Church. For over 2,000 years it has existed. It is all over the world and continues to grow. The Church has lasted through wars, corruption, political turmoil, famines and recessions – because it has deep meaning. It exists to bring together believers to worship the living Jesus Christ. It is not dependent on finance, buildings or structure, just the shared goal of worshiping Jesus. What started with one man, Jesus, and His twelve disciples, is now estimated to include over two billion people.

As Christians, despite how difficult life can get, we have meaning that drives us to carry on – with a heritage of 2,000 years and fellowship with two billion other believers.

**For prayer
and reflection**

Dear Lord, I am so
grateful for all
those who have
gone before me
and those who
currently stand
with me. Thank You
for the privilege of
worshipping You.
Amen.

A life with **purpose**

While in Auschwitz, Victor Frankl used his skills as a psychologist to encourage his fellow prisoners and to help them to find not only meaning, but a purpose. Those in the camp who gave up felt they had no purpose, no reason to carry on. Frankl encouraged them to stop looking to understand why they were in the camp, but instead to focus on what they could do while there. To find a purpose that they imposed on themselves, rather than that which was imposed onto them.

During a job interview, I was surprised to hear the question 'What gets you out of bed in the morning?' On most days, I could honestly say it's the dogs needing to be let out and then fed, the kids needing to get to school, the washing machine needing to be put on and me needing to get to work. This was obviously not the answer the interviewer would have wanted. He would have wanted to know what motivated me; the 'why', not 'what' I did. The real answer would therefore have been my love for my family, my passion for my work and my love for Jesus. This is my underlying purpose and this is the real reason I get out of bed.

Our ultimate purpose is to worship Jesus, but this flows into all areas of our life. God wants us to have life and live life to the full (John 10:10). What does this mean? Are we living abundantly? This does not mean that God promises a full bank account, a big house and fast car, it means finding joy and hope, despite our circumstances, in living our lives filled with purpose. It means finding value and purpose in loving, serving and supporting those around us. When life is about living for Jesus, our whole motivation and opportunities to see joy increase.

1 Peter 2:4–10

'But you are a chosen people… that you may declare the praises of God' (v9)

For prayer and reflection

We looked earlier in the month at our God-given gifts, and then our goals. Spend some time praying and considering your unique purpose as a result of these gifts and goals.

Acceptance

Psalm 139:1–6

'You have searched me, LORD, and you know me.' (v1)

As part of the research into who survived the concentration camps, it was found that the first group of people who did not survive were those who were optimists. They were fine at the start, believing they would be 'out by Christmas', then 'by this time next year'. This helped their ability to cope in the short term, but as time progressed, their optimism left – along with their hope – which proved disastrous. Fixing their focus on the hope of leaving the camp, they hadn't accepted the prospect that they may never leave the camp, or at the very least, would be there for a very long time.

Optimism is a great tool to use in short term, but in order to keep going for the long term, accepting the reality of current situations and circumstances is vital. Although it may be more painful at first, once we have accepted things we are able to keep going longer.

In the same way, although we live with the promise and hope of the wonder of heaven and an eternal life with Jesus, we still need to be able to accept and live in and through whatever life's current challenges and difficulties may be. It helps to know that God is not just our future hope, He is with us in all our situations and circumstances. He knows when we sit and when we rise, He knows our every thought and action, and He will never leave us.

He knows us better than we know ourselves; even the number of hairs on our head. Knowing we can trust Him can bring comfort, particularly when we cannot see a way ahead in a difficult time.

For prayer and reflection

Dear Father, You know every situation and circumstance in my life. Please give me the strength and grace to accept where I am and to keep my faith and hope. Amen.

Contentment

Philippians 4:10–13

'I have learned to be content whatever the circumstances.'
(v11)

Paul wrote his letter to the Philippians while in prison. He wrote about gratitude and contentment, despite his obvious present challenges. In the same way, a common characteristic of those who survived a concentration camp was the ability to find contentment: to find joy, whatever their situation. This may have been by dwelling on a memory of a loved one, watching a bird fly overhead, or noticing a tiny shoot of a plant growing through a crack.

In her book, *The Hiding Place*, Corrie ten Boom details how she was able to practice joy and contentment while in Ravensbrook Concentration Camp. She tells one story of how she and her sister Betsie, despite the most terrible conditions, found joy even from the lice and fleas that swarmed their barracks. The infestation meant the guards wouldn't enter the barracks, and that gave them a certain amount of freedom to read the Bible aloud and pray.

The opposite of contentment is disappointment, sadness, resentment, unrest, frustration, anger and pain. Surely Paul was wise to find the secret to living life well. Contentment meant that he was filled with joy, hope, peace, love and faith despite his unsettling circumstances. If he could find contentment in prison, and Corrie ten Boom could find it in Ravensbrook, then there is every hope that with God's help we too can find contentment whatever our circumstances.

The Bible is filled with instructions to praise God whatever our circumstances (1 Thess. 5:18). No matter what is going on, I have found singing worship songs, or just listening and singing from my heart, dramatically changes everything.

For prayer and reflection

Dear Father, I praise You despite my circumstances. I praise You despite my feelings. I thank You for Your constant love and help. Amen.

Holding on to **values**

Philippians 4:4–9

'whatever is true, whatever is noble, whatever is right … think about such things.' (v8)

In a concentration camp, there was one thing the guards could not take away from a prisoner: their innermost thoughts. No matter what happened, how degraded they were, how cruelly they were treated, they could still have their thoughts and they could still choose to have their values.

In terms of both individuals and organisations, values are the cornerstones. They are the foundations from which we make decisions. Have you ever been in a situation where someone didn't respond to something in the way you expected? It doesn't necessarily mean the way they reacted was wrong; it was just they responded out of a different value system to yours.

Everyone has a value system, even if they've have never taken the time to figure it out. We all have values, and it's quite likely that our friends or people we naturally gravitate towards will probably share a good proportion of them. Today's passage suggests some great values. Skimming through the first half of Philippians 4, we find love, gentleness, thankfulness, peace, honesty, purity, righteousness and excellence.

If we had to reduce the Christian values down to one single core value, it would be love. 1 Corinthians 13 expands this and explains how everything comes out of love. Love is the most powerful word, emotion, value and weapon. We are commanded to love, but it is only because He first loved us and His love is our anchor through the storm. Clinging on to this value of love can help us through life's difficulties.

Do you tend to feel or experience God's love more closely during times of difficulty, or times of ease?

For prayer and reflection

Dear Father, thank You for Your love. Please fill me with it each day, so that I have strength to carry on and can pass on Your love to those around me. Amen.

Next Issue

November

PHILIPPIANS: THE LETTER OF JOY

CATHY MADAVAN

December

THE PROMISE OF ADVENT

JEN BAKER

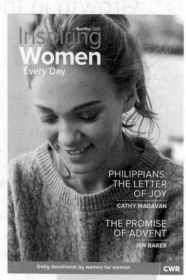

In **November**, Cathy Madavan takes a thematic approach to the letter to the Philippians, and helps us rediscover rejoicing, purpose, unity, and our pursuit of Jesus.

In **December**, Jen Baker anticipates the wonderful promise of Advent by unpacking the prophecy we find in Isaiah 9: 'For unto us, a child is born...'

Also available as eBook/eSubscription

Obtain your copy from CWR, Christian bookshops or your National Distributor.
If you would like to take out a subscription, see the order form at the back of these notes.

Growth in the darkness

....

Psalm 139:7–12

'the night will shine like the day, for darkness is as light to you.' (v12)

Autumn is now here and the nights have drawn in; the long summer evenings are now a distant memory.

The leaves have fallen and the trees may look dead. However, in the darkness, the fallen leaves are now preparing rich soil for new plants and have made way for new leaves that have already started to form, ready to reveal themselves in the spring.

Darkness is often considered negative, yet consider the stars – although always there, they can only be seen at night. A plant can only live due to the formation of the roots and the growth that takes place in darkness.

Our sight is limited in the dark, so we naturally go towards the light. But if we would allow ourselves to walk in the darkness, our eyes would adjust, and we would see more than we thought possible.

God uses the darkness just as much as the light. He created the darkness. We grow in the darkness. Our bodies recover and refresh in the darkness. So embrace God's glory of creation that is evident in the darkness just as much as the light. Do you have any areas in your life that feel like a struggle in the dark? Take another look: is God using this time for you to grow?

....

Optional further reading

Barbara Brown Taylor, *Learning to Walk in the Dark* (Norwich: Canterbury Press, 2015)

A matter of **perspective**

**2 Corinthians
4:16–18**

'So we fix our eyes
not on what is seen,
but on what is
unseen' (v18)

I was recently running a weekly group, focusing on finding tools for positive mental and emotional wellbeing. One of the most useful tools we found for when struggling with something (large or small) was to take time to look at things from a different perspective.

We imagined we could jump into a helicopter and fly up high. While there, we would look at our situation or circumstance to see if we could find additional bits of information that could help us. We would ask questions like: how did this situation come about? Is there an additional resource or extra support that would help resolve it? Is this part of a bigger picture that, now is seen, makes more sense? Changing perspective, widening the focus and seeing the bigger picture always helps.

Several months ago, I was hearing negative words from a member of a committee I lead. As much as we valued his experience and skill, his negativity was unfortunately starting to push the rest of us back, forming stumbling blocks for the wider group. My immediate reaction was to remove his invitation to be part of the committee but, before I did so, with God's help, I 'went up into the helicopter' and looked down. From a different perspective, it became clear to me that he was struggling personally and needed support. My resolve was to privately check in on him. What a turnaround! My attitude completely changed from anger and frustration to concern and love. I thought my asking him was for our benefit, but actually it was for his to be able to receive the support and help that he needed. God's perspective is always the best.

**For prayer
and reflection**

Dear Lord, help me to see with Your eyes, from Your perspective, not only as I deal with my own personal circumstances but also to help those around me. Amen.

Practising the **presence**

Psalm 16:1–11

'I keep my eyes always on the LORD… I shall not be shaken.' (v8)

I n my twenties I learned about Brother Lawrence, a seventeenth-century French monk. Born to disadvantaged parents, to escape poverty he joined the army where he was guaranteed his meals. While there, he experienced God and, following injury, retired and eventually joined a monastery in Paris. Brother Lawrence was given work in the kitchen that was mundane, tedious and repetitive. As he continued his chores of cooking and cleaning, he developed the ability to change his attitude to do all his jobs as if doing them for Jesus. Brother Lawrence turned every act he did into worship: from peeling potatoes, to washing pots, to picking up straw. There was no longer any mundane for him. From that moment on, he did everything out of his love for Jesus; for God's presence. This became known as 'practising the presence of God'.

While learning about Brother Lawrence, we were challenged to find our own simple and mundane moments and change them to become opportunities to practise the presence of God. I chose two things. Every time a phone rings, I allow the first two rings to centre me, to give me a chance to pray for God's presence in my conversation. The second thing is that every time I see a tree, I imagine the stretched-out branches are praising the Lord, and I join in, practising the presence. Other suggestions people came up with were putting dot stickers around their house, car or workplace, so every time they saw them, they were reminded to practise the presence. Since building these triggers into my life, I am grateful they have become firm habits.

For prayer and reflection

What two mundane and simple tasks could you turn into habits that prompt you to practise the presence of God?

Self-compassion

2 Corinthians 1:1–7

'we can comfort those in any trouble with the comfort we ourselves receive from God.' (v4)

What is self-compassion? Let me start by saying what it is not. It is not self-esteem. It is not self-indulgence.

If your best friend was going through a hard time and asked for your help, you wouldn't respond by saying they were silly to get into the situation in the first place, and that they need to toughen up, accept the responsibility and sort it out themselves. But – take a moment here – how often do you talk to yourself that way? We need to demonstrate to ourselves that same compassion we show to others.

So, what *is* self-compassion? What does it look like? Self-compassion means not constantly blaming yourself and putting yourself down for things that have happened outside of your control. Self-compassion means not putting yourself under the pressure of totally unrealistic expectations.

It is treating yourself the way you would your best friend. It is allowing yourself to be loved for who you are, with all your flaws and imperfections, flowing from the love you receive from your loving Father God.

How is this related to resilience? The ability to cope with life can be influenced by what determines our sense of success or failure in the first place. If we set the standard too high, then we are more likely to fall. Practising self-compassion and kindness to ourselves helps to remove the unhelpful self-judgment of unrealistic expectations and standards, and as a result we will not feel the need to bounce back so many times.

As you reflect on this today, is God bringing to mind any particular areas in your own life where you could show yourself some more compassion?

For prayer and reflection

Father, please forgive me for the lack of compassion I have given myself. Thank You that through Your love and kindness, I have all I need to keep going. Amen.

Gratitude

1 Thessalonians 5:12–28

'give thanks in all circumstances; for this is God's will for you in Christ Jesus.' (v18)

One thing I really dislike is whinging. But I was told that if a child whinges, it doesn't mean they aren't grateful (although they may be too young understand gratitude); it is generally a response to the feeling they are not being heard. Once I learned this, I could find solutions, and I was enormously grateful as these stopped the whinging.

Gratitude plays a huge part in being able to build resilience in our lives. The Harvard Mental Health Letter, first published in November 2011,* reports back on the researched carried out by psychologists on two groups. One group was asked to write daily notes of gratitude, while another group was asked to note their irritations. Those who practised gratitude were more healthy and happy. They exercised more, had stronger relationships and generally better outlooks on life.

For some people, being grateful is not something that comes naturally. However, there are ways to build gratitude into your life. An easy step to start with is to begin a gratitude journal. At the end of the day, write down three things you are grateful for. This may be hard to think of at first, but as each day passes, you will notice more and more. Another thing you can do is consciously thank people for what they do, however small. This not only benefits you, but *they* will feel valued and appreciated.

Prayer is also another opportunity to thank God for all that He has done in your life. In challenging ourselves to be thankful to God, we are drawn into gratitude, taking more notice of His extraordinary goodness to us.

To find out more, visit health.harvard.edu

For prayer and reflection

Father, I am so grateful for all You do for me. Please forgive me for the times when when I don't notice the many things You do. Please help me see more of Your love. Amen.

Strength to carry on

Psalm 46:1–7

'God is our refuge
and strength, an
ever-present help
in trouble.' (v1)

We have now spent almost a month looking at the subject of resilience. We know that making mistakes does not make us a failure, it makes us human. We have discovered that God is there in the waiting, in the little simple parts of our lives, wanting us to keep our eyes on Him as His ways are perfect. We have looked at the ability to keep going, to be able to bounce back, to have grit, to develop and grow, to learn to rest and to look after ourselves. We have taken time to look at our God-given gifts, our goals, our life's purpose and ways of practising gratitude. We have delved into research on how people kept going through some of history's toughest times. We have considered Brother Lawrence and explored ways we too can practise the presence of God.

All the way through the month, we have seen, day after day, that God is faithful. God is close to us; He will never leave us. We began the month exploring how we have the invitation to dwell in the shelter of the most high. Today our key verse reminds us that God is our refuge and strength.

I am reminded of the story of Elijah who, despite his amazing victory over the prophets of Baal, still needed a place of refuge in which to build up his strength.

We are all in need, regardless of our position, age, status or experience. Yet at the same time, we can all help. Working together and looking out for one another is one of the joys of being a Christian. Called to be in fellowship, we need one another. So reach out. Encourage your fellow believers today. You're all doing a great job, even though it may not feel like it. You know how the story ends. Keep going. You've got this.

**For prayer
and reflection**

Dear Lord, please
speak to me and
show me ways I
can encourage
others in times of
difficulty. Help me
to direct people to
Your refuge and
strength. Amen.

Weekend

There is always hope

....

Romans 15:1–13

'May the God of hope fill you with all joy and peace as you trust in him' (v13)

When my husband was going through a tough time, we thought it would be a good idea to get him a dog. Not only would it be good company for him, it would encourage him to spend time outside and give him something else to focus on. A few weeks later, our little bundle of fur arrived, and we chose the name Hope, as a positive affirmation for our household. It didn't take long for us to realise the error in the name we chose. Our neighbours must have thought something was very wrong when over the next few weeks we shouted out, 'No Hope!' There would even occasionally have heard us say, 'We've lost Hope.'

Joking aside, 'hope' is the last word relating to resilience that we are going to look at. Hope is saying that everything passes and tough times don't last forever. It is remembering that although we go through storms, difficult situations and circumstances, we have a promised future in Jesus. We have assurance and hope that He will come again, that He will restore all things and create a new heaven and earth. With God, everything is possible. With God, there is always hope.

....

Optional further reflection

Is there someone you know who needs encouragement this weekend, to know that everything passes, nothing lasts forever?

Order form

5 Easy Ways To Order

1. Phone in your credit card order: **01252 784700** (Mon–Fri, 9.30am – 4.30pm)
2. Visit our online store at **cwr.org.uk/store**
3. Send this form together with your payment to: **CWR, Waverley Abbey House, Waverley Lane, Farnham, Surrey GU9 8EP**
4. Visit a Christian bookshop
5. For Australia and New Zealand visit KI Gifts **cwr4u.net.au**

For a list of our National Distributors, who supply countries outside the UK, visit cwr.org.uk/distributors

Your Details (required for orders and donations)

Full Name:	**CWR ID No.** (if known):
Home Address:	
	Postcode:
Telephone No. (for queries):	**Email:**

Publications

TITLE	QTY	PRICE	TOTAL
		Total Publications	

UK P&P: up to £24.99 = **£2.99**; £25.00 and over = **FREE**

Elsewhere P&P: up to £10 = **£4.95**; £10.01 – £50 = **£6.95**; £50.01 – £99.99 = **£10**; £100 and over = **£30**

Total Publications and P&P (please allow 14 days for delivery)	**A**	

Subscriptions* (non direct debit)

	QTY	PRICE (including P&P)			TOTAL
		UK	Europe	Elsewhere	
Every Day with Jesus (1yr, 6 issues)		£16.95	£20.95	Please contact nearest National Distributor or CWR direct	
Large Print *Every Day with Jesus* (1yr, 6 issues)		£16.95	£20.95		
Inspiring Women Every Day (1yr, 6 issues)		£16.95	£20.95		
Life Every Day (Jeff Lucas) (1yr, 6 issues)		£16.95	£20.95		
YP's: 11–14s (1yr, 6 issues)		£16.95	£20.95		
Topz: 7–11s (1yr, 6 issues)		£16.95	£20.95		
Total Subscriptions (subscription prices already include postage and packing)				**B**	

*Only use this section for subscriptions paid for by credit/debit card or cheque. For Direct Debit subscriptions see overleaf.

All CWR adult Bible reading notes are also available in **eBook** and **email subscription** format. Visit **cwr.org.uk** for further information.

Please circle which issue you would like your subscription to commence from:

JAN/FEB   MAR/APR   MAY/JUN   JUL/AUG   SEP/OCT   NOV/DEC

How would you like to hear from us?

Continued overleaf >>

We would love to keep you up to date on all aspects of the CWR ministry, including; new publications, courses and events as well as how you can support us.

If you **DO** want to hear from us on **email**, please tick here [ ]

If you **DO NOT** want us to contact you by **post**, please tick here [ ]

You can update your preferences at any time by contacting our customer services team on 01252 784 700. You can view our privacy policy online at cwr.org.uk

<< See previous page for start of order form

Payment Details

☐ I enclose a cheque made payable to CWR for the amount of: **£** _____

☐ Please charge my credit/debit card.

Cardholder's Name (in BLOCK CAPITALS) _____

Card No. ☐☐☐☐ ☐☐☐☐ ☐☐☐☐ ☐☐☐☐

Expires End ☐☐ ☐☐   Security Code ☐☐☐

Gift to CWR   ☐ Please send me an acknowledgement of my gift   C ☐

Gift Aid (your home address required, see overleaf)

giftaid it I am a UK taxpayer and want CWR to reclaim the tax on all my donations for the four years prior to this year **and on** all donations I make from the date of this Gift Aid declaration until further notice.*

Taxpayer's Full Name (in BLOCK CAPITALS) _____

Signature _____ **Date** _____

*I am a UK taxpayer and understand that if I pay less Income Tax and/or Capital Gains Tax than the amount of Gift Aid claimed on all my donations in that tax year it is my responsibility to pay any difference.

GRAND TOTAL (Total of A, B & C) ☐

Subscriptions by Direct Debit (UK bank account holders only)

One-year subscriptions (6 issues a year) cost £16.95 and include UK delivery. Please tick relevant boxes and fill in the form below.

☐ *Every Day with Jesus*
☐ Large Print *Every Day with Jesus*
☐ *Inspiring Women Every Day*

☐ *Life Every Day* (Jeff Lucas)
☐ *YP's*: 11–14s
☐ *Topz*: 7–11s

Issue to commence from
☐ Jan/Feb ☐ May/Jun ☐ Sep/Oct
☐ Mar/Apr ☐ Jul/Aug ☐ Nov/Dec

CWR Instruction to your Bank or Building Society to pay by Direct Debit

Please fill in the form and send to: CWR, Waverley Abbey House, Waverley Lane, Farnham, Surrey GU9 8EP

DIRECT Debit

Name and full postal address of your Bank or Building Society

To: The Manager _____ Bank/Building Society

Address _____

_____

_____

Postcode _____

Name(s) of Account Holder(s)

_____

Branch Sort Code

☐☐ ☐☐ ☐☐

Bank/Building Society Account Number

☐☐☐☐☐☐☐☐

Originator's Identification Number

4	2	0	4	8	7

Reference

☐☐☐☐☐☐☐☐☐☐☐☐☐☐

Instruction to your Bank or Building Society

Please pay CWR Direct Debits from the account detailed in this Instruction subject to the safeguards assured by the Direct Debit Guarantee. I understand that this Instruction may remain with CWR and, if so, details will be passed electronically to my Bank/Building Society.

Signature(s)

_____

Date

_____

Banks and Building Societies may not accept Direct Debit Instructions for some types of account